EXPANDED UNIVERSES

Christopher Reid was bor[n...] [...] has received some of Brita[in's...] [...] [...]ards, including the Somerset Maugham Award (1980), the Hawthornden Prize (1981) and the Cholmondeley Award (1995), and he is now Poetry Editor at Faber and Faber.

CHRISTOPHER REID

Expanded Universes

faber and faber

LONDON · BOSTON

First published in 1996
by Faber and Faber Limited
3 Queen Square London WC1N 3AU

Photoset by Wilmaset Ltd, Wirral
Printed in England by Clays Ltd, St Ives plc

A CIP record for this book
is available from the British Library

ISBN 0-571-17924-X

10 9 8 7 6 5 4 3 2 1

'The *Universes* were in my 1931 show at the Galerie Percier and were the indirect result of my visit to Mondrian's studio in the Fall of 1930. They weren't intended to move, although they were so light in construction that they might have swayed a little in the breeze . . . The circular forms, particularly interacting, seem to me to have some kind of cosmic or universal feeling. Hence the general title *Universe*. What I would like to have done would have been to suspend a sphere without any means of support, but I couldn't do it.'

ALEXANDER CALDER

Acknowledgements

Many thanks to the editors of the following, in which some of these poems, or versions of them, have appeared: *After Ovid, Fred, Grand Street, Independent, New Poetry Quarterly, New Statesman and Society, New Writing 2, 99 Poems in Translation, The Orange Dove of Fiji, Poetry Book Society Anthology 2, Poetry Book Society Anthology 3, Thumbscrew* and *Times Literary Supplement*. 'Skull Garden' was written for *Ewen Henderson*, a book about the artist. 'Two Dogs on a Pub Roof' was published, with illustrations by Bryan Illsley, as a Prospero Books pamphlet. Twenty-three of the poems were given limited circulation in *Universes* (Ondt & Gracehoper, 1994). 'Dear Diary' was broadcast in a BBC *Bookmark* film, *Love in a Cold Climate*. 'Fetish', 'Epigone' and 'By the By' were read on BBC Radio 4's *Poetry Please!* 'Nature' answered a commission from the Hay-on-Wye Festival of Literature, 1992, for a poem on the theme of 'Communion'. Alexander Calder's words were found in *Calder* by Ugo Mulas and H. Harvard Arnason (Thames and Hudson, 1971).

Contents

Fetish

I have in my possession
an angel's wingbone:
valueless, I gather,
without the certificate
of authentication
which can only be signed by a bishop.

I treasure it, however,
and almost religiously love
the sweet feel of its curve
between thumb and forefinger
deep in my jacket pocket,
the way I'm fondling it now.

Project

A fruitful line of research might be
good manners
in animals.

Start with the big cats:
the jaguar that coughs
before it pounces,
or the one that lays the bones
of its victims in a neat pile
after each meal.

Or again, there's the ounce's
night cry with its
distinct undertone of apology.

Epigone

The last sphinx in captivity
was a disappointing beast,
hardly worthy of the name —
with its unwholesome pelt
like a doubtful
jumble-sale bargain,
and wincing, bloodshot eyes.

All the same,
it was a genuine sphinx
and, once you'd tracked it
to its cage,
could still offer you,
if not some great
poetic riddle to solve,
then at least
a few fairly flabbergasting lies.

From Information Received

In the small crowd
gathered to watch
the mountebank's scandalous
last performance,
there were, I understand,
two people —
a man and a woman —
whose faith in him,.
far from being shattered,
was roundly confirmed.

Detaching themselves
from the crowd's sullen
and self-righteous rhubarb
of disappointment,
they left that dusty
place and took
to the highways and byways,
there to proclaim
the 'good news',
as they insist on describing it.

For, in their opinion,
a miracle did happen:
the fellow did fly,
just as he had said he would,
rapturously rocketing
to some point in the sky
of incalculable altitude,

before seeming
to change his mind
and plunging back earthwards.

To illustrate
their abstruse message,
they have some bit
of business with a stone,
or any handy object,
which they toss in the air,
telling you to fix
your mind on the moment
when it stops and allows
itself to fall.

I don't believe
we need fear this cult,
one among so many
and lacking as it does
either clear moral precepts
or potent symbolism —
some ingenious gimmick
like, say, the cross.
But the usual precautions
might still be in order.

Stones and Bones

SECOND GENESIS

'inde genus durum sumus'
Ovid: *Metamorphoses*, Book I

Two survived the flood.
We are not of their blood,
springing instead from the bones
of the Great Mother — stones,
what have you, rocks, boulders —
hurled over their shoulders
by that pious pair
and becoming people, where
and as they hit the ground.
Since when, we have always found
something hard, ungracious,
obdurate in our natures,
a strain of the very earth
that gave us our abrupt birth;
but a pang, too, at the back
of the mind: a loss . . . a lack . . .

SKULL GARDEN

Ewen Henderson's

For a brief while, you must stand
in this dour patch of land
and draw a deep breath.
Fragrance of life, death
and something more: the sense
of a dark intelligence
determined to conjure the whole
from a pitiless rigmarole
of making and unmaking.
To feel, within you, waking
the same idea that powers
the occasional, upstart flowers,
or drives that twisted tree
through its slow dance, is easy.
But what ancient seed was sown
to yield this crop of stone?
And why all these skulls blooming?
To know that would be something.

By the By

Through a helpful warder,
I soon met the legendary
Dr Spillaine,
author of the *Contradictionary* –
that vast rebuttal
of all established
lexicographical lore.
There was hardly a word
whose accepted meaning
he had not contested
and the whole enterprise rested
on his glorious disdain
for so-called alphabetical order.

Quodlibetical

Think of the energy squandered
in those disputes:
the colour of God's eyes,
or the precise size
of His private parts.
Or wouldn't, as some asserted, those
be otiose?
Even I have wondered.

Moment

For less than a second
on that particular day,
the human dead of the world
numbered precisely the same
as the human living.

Equilibrium . . .

And then a head came
into view, with new thatch
oiled and slickened
against the scalp,
eyes tight and a cry
packed in lungs
ready to tip the whole
dithering edifice
precipitately the other way.

Gossip of the Gods

Haven't you noticed
the difference in quality
between their shadows?

One so strong
and unambiguous,
slapping its blackness
across the floor
as if for a good, long stay.

While the other just flickers there,
dim, irresolute,
at the feet of its owner,
from which you might think
it was yearning, yearning
to slither away.

We shan't know more
without examination
of all contributing factors:
nature of light-source,
atmospheric variables –
that sort of stuff.

Till then, I say,
let's enjoy the peculiar spectacle:
material enough
for infinite titillation,
sniggers galore.

Mermaids Explained

As he read the reports,
he saw at once
that all the mermaids
were dugongs or dolphins.

Their tresses were garlands
of sea vegetation,
or the billows they made
as they swam far off.

And what of the songs
that could lull and lure
impetuous mariners
to their downfall?

A tinnitus compounded
of wind and birds' cries
and something on the brain
too wicked to think about.

A Kind of Poetry

The first empties his pockets
and then builds towers
of the different denominations
to stand by his place at table
while he chews.

The next daydreams
of the death of an imagined relative,
a solicitor's letter the spell
which will change his life.

The third throws most of what he has
at women and flighty horses.

The fourth retains in his nostrils briefly
the faint, print smell
of new notes out of the machine.

Number five never fails to consult
the experts and the stargazers
before attempting
the timidest transaction.

While six, poor six, who must beg for it,
knows just which pitch is lucky
and which not.

Dreaming and Rhyming

You still have the power to haunt.
Last night, you struggled through
pedalling a sort of rickshaw,
family in the back,
down a busy road in France.
You wore a blind man's black
glasses and looked so gaunt,
from the strain and stress and what not,
it took time to see it was you
under that Chinese top-knot.
You have sprung some breathtaking surprises
with your many outlandish disguises,
but this was my first chance
to respond with a suitable kickshaw.

Home

One dog barks
at hot-air balloons
whenever they approach;
another at night-moths.
They are guarding the premises.

Men against Trees

I note that the deforestation of Brazil
    is going ahead at a cracking pace.
Valiant feats of giant-toppling! Disgrace
    to the ancient Empire of Chlorophyll!

Nature's strongholds surrender one by one.
    Even here at home, the fight
continues quietly; men roam about at night
    snapping saplings – and not just for fun.

Burger boxes and buckled lager cans
    stuff the guts of older trees.
On more technical missions, auxiliaries
    steal forth in trucks and vans.

I saw one last week on a daylight job:
    reversing under the boughs of an ash,
he tore a limb and left an enormous gash.
    You had to admire the insouciant slob!

Nature

The gory morsels
television brings
and deposits at our feet,
as the cat her offerings
of punctured mouse,
dishevelled-feathered bird,
leave us too often lost
for the right word.
And so we sit in silence
while across our screen,
through snowdrift and commentary,
gaunt wolverine
go loping in pursuit
of some ill-starred beast
to pluck from its scampering companions,
and the inevitable feast
with its ripping and ravening
is noted by
the ubiquitous camera's
unsparing eye
so matter-of-factly,
and with such a sense
of our being implicated in this,
that no pretence
of horror or detachment
will ever make do
for the lack of a spontaneous
phrase or two

by which to name and greet
the harsh event
and accommodate it between us –
as nature surely meant.

Companion Pieces

A GIFT

It's a terrifying gift,
being able to make you cry,
and when it happens
no one's more shocked than I.

Two or three snatched words
that would seem to have chosen themselves,
flung hastily —
and your whole being dissolves.

I have lost count of the times
I've seen that spasm
destroy the loved lines of your face,
through my iconoclasm.

Like the frenzy of a Roundhead
discharging shot
at an old, carved angel,
and instantly wishing not.

Or (less far-fetched?)
the dazed child who stands
above a broken toy, insisting,
'It jumped out of my hands!'

You could put safe money
on its happening again,
but I've no control at all over it,
so it's your guess when.

AU REVOIR

When you fall ill
you take to your bed,
leaving me to nurse
my own confusion and dread.

Perhaps once a year
you are called away
by some importunate bug
and daren't disobey.

A curt summons,
like wanderlust
it speaks from your very being —
so go you must.

Abruptly, you set out
for the land of ill health,
where you cannot be reached
either by force or by stealth.

Snubbed, bewildered,
I cheat the hours
with superstitious ministrations,
grapes and flowers.

The little nothings
a husband must do,
as he waits for the safe return
of the real you.

Tease

The girl trips
into the lit spot,
displays herself
blatantly there,
then catches her flung clothes
one by one
and puts them on:
dainty panties
and brassière,
old-fangled suspender-belt,
grappled hose,
corset or basque –
all the way
to the final statement,
take it or leave it,
of high heels and furs.

And why do they –
her audience
of connoisseurs,
clapping among the shadows –
submit themselves
time and again
to this ritual,
so elaborately cruel,
of flaunting and withdrawal?
Don't ask.

Dear Diary

Today my wife called me
   a 'pompous old fart'.
We were hugging at the time
   and did not spring apart,
though her words were deliberate
   and struck at my heart.

It's a fearsome business,
   this loving and being loved.
Would anyone try it
   if they hadn't been shoved
by a force beyond resistance,
   velvet-fisted and iron-gloved?

Scenes from Kafka's Marriage

1

A workman came to mend a cupboard door
that would not shut. My wife had got his name
out of the *Yellow Pages*. He did the job
in next to no time, and then, glancing around,
asked if there was anything else he could fix
while he was at it. To be agreeable,
we instantly drummed up a few bits and pieces:
a jittery window-frame, some plastering
and a power-point we hadn't cared to touch
for years. When I took out my wallet to pay him,
he still would not go; in fact, he's here now.
He wanders about the house, just tinkering,
drinks endless mugs of strong, sugary tea
and fills the bathroom with repellent smells.
At night we can't sleep for the noise he makes,
obsessive and rodentlike, with bradawl and screwdriver.

2

I have asked my wife not to argue with me
in public, but I don't think she understands.
This is what I most hate other couples doing:
flaring up at candlelit tables in restaurants,
or grimly bickering in supermarket aisles,
impervious to the flow of loaded trolleys.
To cope with the problem, I have devised a face
which can be switched on at a moment's notice
to cover any possible social shame.
I have practised it for weeks in front of the mirror,

so that, if my wife threatens to embarrass me,
all I shall need to do is to brandish this look,
which is somehow both merry and wise, grave and
    debonair,
and the entire situation will be explained.

3

The theme of last night's dream was infidelity,
although it involved not much more than an episode
of badinage and hand-squeezing with a girl
I had never met before, but whose piquant, freckled
plainness made me feel especially tender.
When I woke up, I wanted the feeling to last
and so I told my wife just what had happened,
only putting her in this strange girl's place.
It was a bad mistake. She grew suspicious
and I at once started to ornament my narrative
with ever more spurious and irrelevant details,
either invented or borrowed from other dreams.
Of course, this served to make things far worse.
It seems unfair, not being able to turn
one's involuntary flights of fancy to domestic advantage.

Feathers

After the big fire
at the feather factory,
the whole city
fell under a thick
cloud of feathers.
The boisterous guffaw
of the conflagration
had boosted them skywards,
and there they hung –
a gentle, indecisive blizzard
for most of a week.
Just to step out of doors
was to hazard
feathers in your hair,
in your eyes, up your nostrils,
on the blade of your tongue.
Pollution or sacrament?
The cleverest minds of the day
applied themselves
and a hundred quibbling
tracts and sermons
were written and distributed.
The incorporeality
and feathers together
to some suggested
angels, exaltation,
a new order;
to others, anarchy, death . . .
Then it began to clear.
But even when that turmoil

had subsided,
the last of the feathers
trodden into a mush
like old snow,
for a while at least
some something in the air
continued to dangle and vex us.

After Mallarmé

A lace curtain self-destructs
in its supremely uncertain
fling at exposing only
the shock of a bed's final absence.

The concerted all-white internecine
fight of this hanging thing
dashed against a wan pane
flutters more than it lays to rest.

Under the dreamer's golden canopy, though,
there languishes a lute
with its deep musical emptiness

which turned towards a window
could from its belly alone
give birth to you like a son.

Fly

A fat fly fuddles for an exit
at the window-pane.
Bluntly, stubbornly, it inspects it,
like a brain
nonplussed by a seemingly simple sentence
in a book,
which the glaze of unduly protracted acquaintance
has turned to gobbledygook.

A few inches above where the fly fizzes
a gap of air
waits, but this has
not yet been vouchsafed to the fly.
Only retreat and a loop or swoop of despair
will give it the sky.

Cycle

As she proffered
that enormous gin and tonic,
the clink of ice-cubes jostling
brought to mind
an amphitheatre
scooped from a sun-lulled hillside,
where a small breeze carried
the scent of lemon-trees
and distant jostle of goat-bells,
bringing to mind
an enormous gin and tonic.

Insofar

Put on this earth to sleep,
but with no true calling for the deep

problems of utter forgetfulness
or the lurid and scary mess

of my dreams, I have deemed it wise,
insofar as I can, to specialise

in those moments on the brink
when the brain is too tired to think

but moves, still, to a chant, or thud,
that could be the song of my blood

or some rhythm borrowed from the prose
of a book dropped as eyes close

and I pass, alertly swooning,
into a sort of pebble-beach communing

with the great blur of the sea:
a modulation almost visionary,

like finding myself in a land
whose language I do not understand

but from which I could bring back
some wisdom, some purloined knack,

just so long as I keep
it safe from the snatches, the deep

inveiglements of sleep.

Reflection

The two males meet
in a complicated crash,
disengage, retreat
and, with less panache

than began this day
of hatstand-duelling,
swerve back to the fray.
The contest is gruelling,

the prize unclear:
king of the herd
till what — next year?
But which is more absurd:

these frenziedly rutting
beasts in their scrimmage,
or me head-butting
my mirror-image

(my only rival,
as I sit here fighting
for the doubtful survival
of some quaint, rhymed writing)?

Intelligentsia

The whole world knows Gertrude,
from the prose-style
to the hairstyle.
Even Hem's embittered
and disloyal portrait
in *A Moveable Feast* will
never diminish that versatile
genius.
       Leo, too, is celebrated
according to his deserts.

But what of Phyllis, their sister,
who loathed all the arts
and would 'sooner die than look at a picture'?

Isn't it time we heard more
about her?

First It Killed the Romans

O table!
O preposterous vocative!
The first giggle
Latin surprised us with –
seven years old
and not yet in awe
of the implications
of such an unlikelihood:
of Gayev, for instance,
buttonholing that piece of wood,
his family bookcase;
or me now face to face
with the four-legged friend,
scored and stained,
I use as my writing-desk,
conjuring up the treble
uproar of a classroom
thirty-five years ago . . .

O table!

One for the Footnotes

Born in Hong Kong in 1949,
Christopher Reid was soon observed to shine
in the fields of nappy-wetting and ululation.
The leading baby of his generation,
he founded what became known as the Infantile School,
whose principal tenet, scorn for every rule,
inspired a brief literary Pentecost.
Sadly, his early efforts are now lost,
as is his output from the next two years
of experimentation with bawling, tantrums, tears
and other non-verbal forms of expression. The lure
of words, however, distracted him from this pure
line of enquiry, and one can only regret
his falling under the spell of the alphabet,
which led to such work of his as survives: obscene
botches, travesties of what might have been.

Eight Octets

A haven of lorn hotels, the square
wakens to a chorus of fried-bread breakfasts.

The pungent sizzle hangs like a mist;
cutlery and crockery clatter in the basements.

Lit windows show where consciousness resumes:
known clothes pulled on in alien rooms.

Above the roofline, a London sky
begrudges daylight as I walk to work.

A TRACT FOR THE MILLENNIUM

We no longer have queues,
only competitive waiting.

Citizens fret in a scrimmage
until whenever the bus turns up.

That old woman's tongue tuts
with more threat than the tick of a time-bomb.

After you, madam! After you, sir!
I'm in no hurry.

WIPED

Time flies faster than ever.
I fall asleep on the train up to London
and the journey seems to take fifteen minutes.
Where did that hour go?

In galloping dreams whose tails I tried
to catch, but couldn't, as I was waking:
memory wiped, and in its place
the grogginess that follows anaesthesia.

DUTCH UNCLE

The stupid, plotless opera
of brats and babies
continues downstairs.

Up here, the door snicks shut
on monkish quiet.

God's in His heaven;
waterpipe and cistern
companionably gurgle.

INCLUDE ME OUT

Pastoral manifestation of the military,
the bandstand band blows Sunday afternoon away:
old tunes you jolt yourself now and then not to fall into step
    with.
But why not be affable, this once, and obey?

Bunting receives the breeze with a visible frisson
and all the flowerbeds go hooray.
Only you, it seems, persist in your dogged slouching and
    glowering.
Only you won't play.

DISPLACEMENT BLUES

The clock of the body
is out of kilter again:
a longitudinal lurch
has jarred its works
and it won't be right for days now.
Until then,
I must orbit the city
like a moon around the wrong planet.

SOMEHOW

The vibraphone's high-speed rubber ice-cubes,
the clarinet's lickety-split,
piano and drums dapper and dangerous under them —
and somehow they all fit!

The track skedaddles faster than I can follow,
leaving a brief space
for the urge to be better, cleverer, righter somehow:
illusions of grace.

NOCTURNAL

Once more, galvanic insomnia
comes to devastate the small hours.

Death is the one big fact there,
stark as a standing stone.

In counter-argument, pulses
the perishable filament of selfhood.

A pilgrimage of waiting may bring you
to either brief sleep or daybreak.

Distance

If I peer down from my desk
and into the walled yard
where the tinies are left to play
most of each weekday,
I am pretty certain to see
some sort of bother:
one mite hitting another,
or shoving or tripping or wrestling
him or her over,
the better to plant a good kick.

Look, something's happening now:
a bloblet in knitted gloves,
gumboots and anorak
does not appreciate
that, inches behind her back,
some like creature is lifting
a yellow pedal-car
almost as big as he is
and will soon be bringing it down
on her frail pate.

Lawlessness, cruelty, woe . . .
The whole set-up's grotesque,
but there's no point in my shouting.
With traffic between, and a shut window,
it's too far from this desk.

Night Games

In playground and park,
   we have giggling and anarchy.
Evenings fall dark
   and the whole town turns panicky.

A new, mocking light
   in the eyes of our children
fills us with fright:
   their behaviour's bewildering.

Like an upstart army
   of imps and jokers,
they are driving us barmy
   with their hocus-pocus.

Now what's gone wrong?
   What's the matter,
that they treat us all night long
   to this eerie satire?

What does it mean,
   this bumptious violence –
all the more obscene
   for its cloak of shadows and silence?

As the sun sinks down,
   toddlers and teenagers
spill across town
   expending their energies.

Night becomes at once
  an unruly circus
for the attitudes and stunts
  most likely to shock us.

Caught up in a swarm
  that grows ever more dangerous,
our little ones transform
  to unbiddable strangers.

Hurtling blind
  in and out of the darkness,
they exhibit every kind
  of friskiness and larkiness.

And the moon casts its glow
  on the field of idiocy,
picks out tableaux
  and highlights them hideously.

So, wherever we look,
  we see allegorical
images from some nightmare book,
  after Bosch or Bruegel.

The same charade
  is repeated each evening;
then why should it be so hard
  to catch the meaning?

These truculent japes,
  this hectic tumbling
and milling and shifting of shapes
  must signify something.

Or has some devil taught
  our perfectly ordinary
offspring this cruel sport,
  this buffoonery?

Our love and sadness
  prompt the question
whether an incurable madness
  has possessed them.

Or may a child
  yet subdue the demon
that bids it run wild
  over waste plot, churchyard and common?

As the small hours lurch by
  and they grow tireder,
till some look about to die,
  things get weirder.

Forsaking the open spaces
  to crouch in corners,
they show us the faces
  of inconsolable mourners.

Because we yearn to understand
  or feel less distant,
we hold out a hand —
  always too hesitant.

For instantly mouths gape wide
  and a species of cackling
from deep inside
  greets us like heckling.

And off they fly once more,
    as tantalising
and as heartless as before,
    till dawn reinstates the horizon.

The Thing and the Book

I wrote a thing in a book
which some people did not like,
and so they decided to kill me.
Now I have gone into hiding,
though I cannot escape my fear.
Shall I ever be free again?

Let me say it again:
I wrote a thing in a book
and now I must live in fear.
What will it be like,
to spend my entire life hiding?
Would it have been kinder to kill me?

They certainly wanted to kill me,
to kill me again and again.
But now I am in hiding,
so instead they must kill my book –
not the same thing, but something like –
and make the most of my fear.

Possibly they hope the fear
will be enough to kill me.
That is what they would like,
before I can do it again:
write some other book
deserving of a good hiding.

You might suppose they were hiding
their own, bigger fear —
fear of the power of a book —
in all this effort to kill me.
It won't be much of a gain,
but think that, if you like.

I don't believe that's what it's like.
I hope we're not on a hiding
to nothing, but time and again
I return to my deepest fear
that, even if they fail to kill me
and do not destroy my book,

no book so feared or disliked
will ever again find a hiding-place.
So they might as well kill us all.

Two Dogs on a Pub Roof

There are two dogs on a pub roof.
One's called Garth, the other Rolf.
Both are loud – but don't think they're all mouth.
I've been watching them and it's my belief
that they've been posted there, not quite on earth,
as emissaries of some higher truth
it's our job to get to the bottom of,
if only we can sort out the pith from the guff.
Garth's bark's no ordinary *woof, woof*:
it's a full-throttle affair, like whooping-cough,
a racking hack that shakes him from scruff
to tail in hour-long binges of holding forth
on all manner of obsessive stuff,
from pigeons and planes to not getting enough
to eat and so being ready to bite your head off.
He's whipped up in a perpetual froth
of indignation on his own behalf.
Poof! Dwarf! Oaf! Filth!
These and suchlike are among his chief
forms of salutation – and he means you, guv!
His whole philosophy, his pennyworth,
is 'All's enemy that's not self'
(with the provisional exception of his brother Rolf).
It's no joke and you don't feel inclined to laugh.
Rolf's even more frightening: his *arf! arf!*
seems designed to tear the sky in half,
every utterance an ultimate expletive,
every one a barbed shaft
aimed accurately at your midriff
and transfixing you with impotent wrath.

You and him. It bothers you both.
The thing's reciprocal, a north-south
axis that skewers the two of you like love.
You're David and Goliath, Peter and the Wolf,
Robin Hood and his Sheriff, Mutt and Jeff —
any ding-donging duo from history or myth
that's come to stand as a hieroglyph
for eternal foedom, non-stop strife,
the old Manichean fisticuffs
without which there'd be no story, no life,
and the whole cycle of birth, breath,
scoff, boff, graft, grief and death
would amount to so much waste of puff.
You're spiritual partners, hand in glove,
you and Rolfie, you and Garth,
you and the two of them up on that roof,
barking and hopping, acting tough,
flinging their taunts across the gulf
of the entire neighbourhood: *You lot down beneath!*
You got a diabolical nerve!
Who gave you permission to breathe?
This is our gaff! This is our turf!
Don't even think of crossing our path,
if you happen to value what remains of your health!
One false move and we'll show you teeth . . .
And so on. Of course, that's only a rough
translation, but it will more or less serve,
being at least the gist of the riff
that bores you mad and drives you stiff
all day long. Night, too. Nights, they work shifts.
One sleeps, while the other faces the brave
task of keeping the moon at a safe
distance and making sure the stars behave.

Which is why there are two of them. If
you've begun to wonder. As you no doubt have.
Then sometimes they'll mount an all-night rave,
Garth dancing with Rolf, Rolf with Garth —
though there's nothing queer about these two
    psychopaths —
and you're the inevitable wallflower, on the shelf,
surplus to requirements. Only you can't stay aloof.
Like it or lump it, you're stuck in their groove.
The joint's jumping in every joist and lath
and nobody, but nobody, is going to leave.
You're as free an agent as the flame-fazed moth
that's in thrall, flamboyantly befuddled, and not fireproof.
You're party to the party, however loth.
You belong along. You're kin. You're kith.
You're living testimony to the preposition 'with'.
You're baby, bathwater and bath.
So don't dash out with your Kalishnikov
and hope to cut a definitive swathe
through the opposition. Don't throw that Molotov
cocktail. Put down that Swiss Army knife.
Stop spitting. Stop sputtering. Don't fluster. Don't faff.
And don't be so daft, naff, duff or uncouth
as to think you're calling anyone's bluff —
let alone that of the powers above —
by threatening to depart in a huff.
They are your world, where you live,
and this is what their telegraph
of yaps and yelps, their salvoes of snuff-
sneezes, their one-note arias, oath-
fests and dog-demagoguery, their throes of gruff
throat-flexing and guffaws without mirth
are meant to signify. And it's all for your behoof!

So thanks be to Garth, and thanks to Rolf —
those two soothsayers with their one sooth,
pontificating on that pub roof —
and thanks to the God who created them both
for your enlightenment and as proof of His ruth!

Cardboard

In this great, new city of ours
not only the dwellings,
but the roads are, too;
the very foundations
and the entire
infrastructure
of ducts and cables;
the guts; the works . . .

Already our sewer-pipes exhibit
dropsical swellings;
pavements are trodden to pulp
after the lightest
of summer showers;
the blocks and towers
of banks and offices
sag and sway,
inexorably losing their glue.

And what do the powers
propose to do?
Well, last week they permitted
a two-minute interview
with a life-size replica
of the minister.
Who was pressed hard,
but he certainly wasn't telling us.